MORRISTON
THEN & NOW
IN COLOUR

ANDRÉ SCOVILLE

The History Press

*This book is dedicated to my hubby
John Charles Barrett who has become an
adopted 'Morriston Monkey' through his
interest and the knowledge that I have
forced upon him for over a decade.*

First published in 2014

The History Press
The Mill, Brimscombe Port
Stroud, Gloucestershire, GL5 2QG
www.thehistorypress.co.uk

British Library Cataloguing in Publication Data.
A catalogue record for this book is available from the British Library.

ISBN 978 0 7524 9350 3

Typesetting and origination by The History Press
Printed in India.

CONTENTS

FOREWORD

'I alone cannot change the world, but I can cast a stone across the waters to create many ripples.'

Mother Teresa

It is a great privilege and honour to write this foreword to André's new book. Coming from Morriston myself and now working as the Vicar of St David's, I have seen many changes in our community. For example, the school I attended (Martin Street) is no longer there but through my work I now visit the nursing home on the site, and the swimming pool in Morriston park where many of us spent happy summers is long gone. Just two examples of how our community has changed over the years.

Morriston is a community that has a very interesting past – through heavy industry, the shopping centre, and importantly the people who have shaped our community.

All of us will have our own story and memories of buildings, people and events that we have encountered.

Like many, I have bought André's previous books as they have been published over the years, and greatly enjoyed looking at and learning from the pictures and careful details André puts into his books.

André Scoville (Morriston Archivist and Historian) has a wealth of knowledge about our town and its people, and we are privileged that he has taken the time to bring to us the history and images contained within this book.

The images I am sure will stir up memories in all Morristonians as each picture tells the story of the social, economic and personal change that has taken place, and how the Morriston we know today has been shaped by its past, whilst looking at the role we have to play in shaping it for its future.

Reverend Hugh Lervy
Vicar of Morriston & Area Dean of Cwmtawe

INTRODUCTION

It has been an immense pleasure compiling the photographs and writing this book, because I know it will be valued by all ages as they see how Morriston has changed over the years. It is slightly different to other books that I have had published, in as much as that all of the photographs are in colour. Choosing the 'then' photographs was a difficult task, as I wanted to cover as much of Morriston and its surrounding villages as possible – my only issue was the amount of old colour photographs in my archive that I could contrast to how the scene looks today.

Morriston is a town steeped in history and so much more than will fit within this book. We have come a long way since the mines and tinplate works disappeared from our horizon. Morriston has become quite a shop- and office-based community; gone are the engine houses and the numerous chimneystacks that for many generations once stood firm on our landscape.

However, although the town is cleaner by environmental terms, it has had its casualties; in recent years Morriston has lost too many of its public houses and landmark buildings. We do not deserve the boarded up and decaying buildings after years of pollution from the industries of the day. Visitors might say that Morriston is shabby-looking and, in parts, they are correct, but that is only the aesthetic surface. Look deeper and you will see that the people have not really changed. It is still a working-class town with working-class values. The people of Morriston care and grow to love Morriston; the character of the town is still the same. The original grid layout from William Edwards' plan remains and so too does the oldest place of worship, Libanus. The River Tawe still flows while we hang on to the church in the middle of the road, the former St John's, which is now in private ownership.

It is my aim to tell you something that you did not already know about Morriston, to evoke some memories in established residents and give new to the town an insight into how we used to look – not always for the better! Unfortunately, there is so much history and so many funny stories that I had to leave out due to lack of space. Ask me about them and I can guarantee to have you laughing and crying at the same time.

This book is a dedication to past and present Morristonians who have loved the town almost as much as me. I have to thank the people that support what I do, either by my rapidly growing Facebook page (www.facebook.com/MrMorriston), which was the first Morriston-orientated page to reach 1,000 'likes' (and it did so in just ten weeks), or by thanking me for my work when they meet me. The encouragement of my supporters drives me to continue on this path of archiving this beautiful town in any capacity that I can, something that I have been doing for the past thirty years, and recently under the name of Mr Morriston.

André Scoville, 2014

GENERAL VIEW
OVER MORRISTON

DOMINATING EACH PHOTOGRAPH is the striking and unique Chapel of Nonconformity, Tabernacle Chapel, which was about to celebrate its 100th anniversary a year after the early photograph was taken in 1971, which has an active industrial setting as well as a

religious one. The Morganite carbon factory is being extended, which was eventually opened officially by the Duchess of Kent on 12 October 1971. Opposite the construction site of Morganite, you can see the bricked-up windows of the Dyffryn Tinplate Works; this site has amassed many wild trees today. The three houses with whitewashed back walls that are in the early photo were on Graig Terrace. They were demolished in 1989 due to landslide problems in that area.

THE COMPARISON PHOTO shows a 'green' Morriston, the trees having been planted in gardens at Crown and Morfydd streets. The Morganite site has now been scaled down and replacing much of the works is Asda hypermarket, which opened on 5 July 1999; two fast-food restaurants, Taybarns restaurant and a Premier Inn. The garages on the Wagg-fach (otherwise known as the Wac or Old Engine House) have gone; the land having been sold at auction recently with planning consent for residential use. Rees & Kirby's Victoria Yard at Neath Road is now a boarded-up Aldi. Use Tabernacle Chapel and St John's Church (in the middle of the road) as a guide and you will not go wrong.

BEDFORD HOUSE

ONCE THE MORRISTON headquarters of the Royal British Legion, the early photograph was taken in 1994 before the building became empty and caught fire. It was demolished in 1997. Nine one-bedroomed flats for disabled people were later built on the site. Daniel Edwards, Justice of the Peace Magistrate, lived at Bedford House towards the end of his life, an ideal location to view the famous Tabernacle Chapel where he managed the builders in 1870. Edwards was employed by Richard Hughes in 1859 in management at the Upper Forest Tinplate Works (now the site of an Asda supermarket). Unfortunately, he was found to be recording the secret methods and ideas of Hughes' tin production, with the intention of establishing the Dyffryn Tinplate Works (which he did in 1874). When his actions were discovered, he was instantly dismissed.

In retaliation, Daniel Edwards, by now in charge of the building work for Tabernacle Chapel, ensured that the full name of Richard Hughes' daughter was omitted from the

carving in the foundation stone of the newly constructed chapel – her full name is still missing to this day: Miss Annie Hughes (Morfydd Glantawe).

Edwards need not have sought revenge because the Landore Tinplate Works, where Hughes was a managing partner, ran into financial difficulty partly due to the large company established by Daniel Edwards. Richard Hughes was declared bankrupt in December 1892. He was forced to move from a lavish country house in Ynystawe to Rock House at Neath Road, which is still there today next to Morriston Primary School. He became a neighbour to Daniel Edwards who lived at Morfydd House at the time (situated next to his unlived-in Danbert Hall).

ON 8 OCTOBER 1911, Mrs Ann Edwards, wife of Daniel Edwards, who was now a retired tinplate manufacturer, left her husband £12,818 0s 9d in her will. When Daniel passed away on 28 December 1915, he left a considerably reduced sum of £2,759 12s to his sons Ebenezer Gwyn Edwards (described as a 'Gentleman') and Richard Gwyn Edwards ('Solicitor'). When another of Daniel Edwards' sons, William Henry Edwards, died just four years after his father after taking ownership of the Dyffryn Tinplate Works, he left £770,597 16s 11d to a family member.

THE BEVANS ARMS PUBLIC HOUSE

THE 1974 PHOTOGRAPH shows The Bevans Arms and the vacated premises of Uriel Rees Ironmongers, which was established in 1870. It is now an intermittent furniture shop – with one furniture shop closing to be replaced by another furniture shop due to its size.

Named after William Bevan, The Bevans Arms was originally a bank. The first savings bank in Glamorgan was established in Morriston by the Quaker philanthropist William Bevan, who acted as its first treasurer, with Sir John Morris serving as its first president. By 1829, this institution had accumulated balances from depositors worth no less than £9,209, worth £820,000 in today's money. The Morriston bank was early in the field in Wales, and was absorbed by the Swansea Savings Bank in 1829.

MONEY CONTINUED TO pass between hands when the building took on the name of The Bevans Arms. A meeting was scheduled at the public house for 13 July 1903 in order to discuss a proposal to seek a reduction in tram fares between Morriston and Swansea, but although many residents had strong opinions, the meeting was not opened because only a few people actually turned up.

Many landlords have called time at Bevans, including David Jenkins, in the 1860s; William Thomas, in the 1880s; Robert and Winifred Wright in the 1930s; and around 1949–60 the pub was being run by Philip and Frances James. The pub closed in 2007 and has remained closed ever since.

CALFARIA WELSH BAPTIST CHAPEL

PICTURED HERE IN 1986, Calfaria Welsh Baptist Chapel was formed by fifty-eight members who attended Seion Chapel's Sunday school at Wychtree Street. The foundation stone was laid in 1885 and it was officially opened on Sunday, 11 March 1888 with seats for 700 people. The first minister was William Lewis (1858–1890), who proved to be a great leader within the Wychtree Sunday school. He had already served Seion as an occasional preacher combining his ministry with his job as a labourer at the Beaufort Tinplate Works, but now he was full-time within the new Calfaria. Within two weeks, he had baptised twenty-seven people and accepted them as members of the new chapel. A year later, local MP Sir Henry Hussey Vivian was invited to open the chapel, at which point the membership had increased to 260 people. Some Sunday evenings, up to 400 people listened to William Lewis preaching in

Calfaria. Sadly, as the chapel went from strength to strength, William Lewis was struck down with kidney disease and he died in June 1890, aged 33, leaving a wife and four infant children. He was buried along the main path of Seion Chapel's cemetery in Clase Road.

AS THE YEARS went by, membership numbers fluctuated and the ministers changed. Chapel debt had reached £2,983 by 1933 and the minister at the time volunteered to accept a reduction in pay although the chapel's debt would not be cleared completely until March 1946. It seems that the late 1950s was a happy time in Calfaria; the chapel was painted and refurbished throughout, a gas heating system had been installed and there was a strong youth fellowship, but as they say, 'all good things must come to an end'. In early 1973, discussions between the Welsh Baptists at Seion, Soar, Calfaria and Tabernacle in Cwmrhydyceirw concluded with the decision to share the ministry, thus saving money on individual ministers. Tabernacle in Cwmrhydyceirw eventually pulled out leaving the other three to think about forming a single church and, following an architect's report, Seion was agreed to be the most appropriate chapel for the new merger. Calfaria closed in 1981 and although the building was used for some time as the practise room for the Morriston Orpheus Male Voice Choir, it was eventually demolished in 1991. The land has remained unused ever since.

CANAL

THE OLD PHOTOGRAPH is of the canal at Neath Road taken in 1954, which now forms part of the Neath Road bypass. The whole of the Swansea Canal took four years to complete (1794–8) and was the biggest engineering project undertaken in Swansea in the eighteenth century. At Morriston in 1849, a lot of the drinking water came directly from the canal and weir at Wychtree; cholera and other diseases were rife, and people were ignorant of the fact that their tea and beer was brewed with this filthy water. It was said in jest that you were not a true Morristonian until you had fallen in the canal. Those that remember the canal recall rats and dead animals, and desperately trying not to swallow any of the water as they fell in. However, on a serious note, many children drowned in the canal throughout its lifetime.

Four-year-old David John Williams of No. 1 Nixon Terrace was discovered floating face down in the canal on Saturday, 15 August 1903. It seemed he had dropped a halfpenny into the canal the day before and wanted to get it out. The coroner blamed mothers for gossiping at doors instead of attending to their children. Two-year-old Thomas Stuart Sprake of No. 22 Clyndu Street was drowned in the canal on Monday, 12 May 1952. The coroner recorded an open verdict, as there was no evidence at all to show how he fell into the canal. Draining of the canal started in May 1970 with Swansea Council receiving a grant towards diverting the canal water into the River Tawe.

THE SECTION OF the canal in the older photographer was replaced by grassy banks and Neath Road was widened with the demolition of many old houses. By 1990, the need for a bypass was great, as Swansea Enterprise Park had become a major part of Morriston with immense queues on the old Neath Road and Wychtree roundabout. The Morriston Wychtree interchange and Neath Road underpass and bypass cost £35 million. Pensioners Mr David Jones from Tircanol Post Office and Mrs Dilys Davies of Bedford Street opened it on 19 November 1996 at 3.05 p.m. This was able to happen ten weeks ahead of schedule due to the tolerant and co-operative approach of residents towards the necessary work carried out by Nuttall's contractors. The opening was followed by refreshments at the Red Lion public house.

CHURCH STREET
(LOWER MORFYDD STREET)

THE EARLY PHOTOGRAPH dates to 1915 when the street housed many of the gentry's residences. On the left is Dyffryn Villa and, although it is officially on Davies Street, it links very well to Morfydd House on the right of the photos because both of the buildings were the residence of Daniel Edwards (JP) who was titled a 'Pioneer of Morriston Industry' by the *South Wales Daily Post* when he died in December 1915. As previously mentioned, he founded the Dyffryn Tinplate Works and was responsible for overseeing the builders of Tabernacle Chapel.

A LITTLE FURTHER up behind the garden of Dyffryn Villa was The Poplars, which later served Morriston well by becoming Morriston Clinic and Dr Paul Mellor's GP Practice until it moved to Sway Road in July 1989. The building was demolished in 1994 and on its site is now Jim Havard Court. Danbert Hall (aka Dunbar House) is on the right of the photo, which is next door to Morfydd House. The terrace on the right in the foreground of the new photo was named Rock Terrace as it was built on the land belonging to Rock House (corner of Lower Morfydd Street and Neath Road), but confusion arises between Rock Terrace here and the one near Treharne Road which kept its name. In 1900, No. 1 Church Street was occupied by the Morriston branch of the Glamorgan Banking Company Limited.

CLYNDU STREET

THE OLDER OF the two images is the top of Clyndu Street in 1962, and shows how it looked nine years prior to Swansea Council's compulsory purchase of all of the houses on the right side of the street in order to widen the road. The Old Prince public house dates back to 1869, when Mr John Jones was the proprietor. Thirty-three years later, it had changed hands and was run by Mr William Tucker. He invited John Jones back to the Old Prince for a presentation on behalf of the 'Loyal T.H. Griffiths' Lodge' where John Jones was one of its most zealous members and promoters. He was honoured by the council of the Lodge by being presented with its emblem containing John Jones' portrait. The singing was

reported to have been meritorious as it was unassisted by any instrument. It appears that Morriston was in fine voice, even in those days.

It is largely unknown that underneath Clyndu Street is the Clyndu Mining Canal, which could have been constructed as early as 1747/48 and was used for transporting coal to the copper works near the Duke. It is suggested that the water from the mile-long canal also helped to manage the mills at the Forest Copperworks. The wasteland adjacent to the lower part of Clyndu Street housed the Clyndu steam-engine house.

It seems that by 1846 the underground canal had not been used for a long time and towards the end of its working life was only used to empty the water from Clyndu Colliery.

MAYBE, THIS WILL explain the amount of water that can be heard underneath the ground when standing at the top of Morfydd Street, not to mention the water flowing down many of the streets at this part of Morriston after rain has fallen.

CROSS TOWARDS CLASE ROAD – 1908

THE OLDER IMAGE is a charming view of Morriston Cross at the turn of the twentieth century, with the original Lamb & Flag public house on the left along with an ironmongers and The Cross Inn on the right. Sadly, The Cross Inn closed its doors for the final time in January 2013 after more than 160 years of trading (apart from a brief spell during 1994–96 when it was renamed The Rat & Carrot). The road one can see in the older photograph was originally called Llangyfelach Road later becoming Clase Road, and Pentrepoeth Road is behind the photographer. We can see a newsagent with the daily news on boards propped on his shop window. For nearly eighty years, this was a newsagent. The separate businesses were Thomas's (*c.* 1909–50); Billy Hole, in addition to his Tours & Private Party Outings (*c.* 1950–75) and Alan Hole, the son of Billy Hole and an ex-Swansea Town

footballer (*c.* 1975–88). Alan then relocated the business to the former Albany Furniture Shop at No. 138 Woodfield Street where he remained until 2006 under the name of Good News.

MUCH OF MORRISTON CROSS was rebuilt in 1903–04 replacing 'dilapidated' whitewashed cottages with many of the red-brick buildings that can be seen today, such as The Cross Inn. However, when motor vehicles started appearing on the main streets in Morriston, the Swansea Corporation had major concerns. The Morriston streets that extended from the original grid layout were small, narrow lanes with scattered housing in an unconventional layout and a lack of pavement as there had been no need for them previously. Because of this, 1930–32 saw major changes to these roads as the council purchased land, demolished buildings and laid out full-sized roads, wide enough to accommodate three lanes of traffic and pavements on each side. Morriston was modernised ready for the traffic that it sees today. The original building of the Lamb & Flag public house was demolished and replaced by a building of art deco design with 1932 marked clearly at the top. Whitewashed cottages that survived the 1903/4 demolition, situated on the corner of Woodfield Street and Clase Road, were also demolished for an unusual and striking replacement of the 'round buildings' suitably named as the New Cross Buildings.

21

CROWN STREET

ONE HUNDRED YEARS apart and hardly anything has changed when we compare Upper Crown Street of 1912 to the same view today. Crown Street is aptly named after one of Morriston's oldest public houses, The Crown Inn. It dates back to 1856 when John Williams was the proprietor; he brewed his own beer, probably in the outer building seen in the older photograph. The Crown Inn has had a colourful past, which saw the inevitable happen in 2012, when it was closed and boarded up. On 16 January 1971, the landlord, Mr Morgan Miles, was found dead after a fire broke out in an upstairs kitchen. He had been managing the pub for twenty years. His wife Doris Miles was rescued by firefighters. If it was not for their neighbour, Mr Dennis Baglow at No. 22, who called the fire brigade and broke down a side door, the outcome may have been even worse for her.

THE LARGE HOUSE on the left of the photographs was at one time a doctors' surgery. Many residents will remember Drs Williamson, Pugh and Murray practicing here throughout the 1940s to mid-1980s. Further on up on the opposite side of the road at No. 15 was Crown Printers owned by John Jones & Son, which was the original name for the printers. They were well established in the Swansea area, having started in 1890. They were situated at the back of Nos 15–19 Crown Street. After the printers closed its doors for the last time, the premises were occupied for many years by Darglen Motors, until it moved to Neath Road. Today, Crown Auto Repairs occupy the premises.

CHEMICAL WORKS

THE CLEARED SITE of Pentrepoeth Chemical Works in 1986. The image is in complete contrast to the houses that now occupy the site called Llys Dol, off Chemical Road. The works were opened in 1860 by David Thomas, a grocer of Church Street (now Lower Morfydd Street), but after various partnership dissolutions in 1866 and 1870, the company was bought by F.W. Berk & Co. At 10.30 a.m. on 9 August 1903, considerable damage was caused to the main buildings when a fire broke out in the drying room. Information reached Inspector Parker at the police station and basic fire appliances were sent to the scene. A hydrant was located that provided a good supply of water, but the fire spread so rapidly that the Swansea fire brigade were called upon. They arrived with Sergeant Edwards, and following in a horse and trap was Captain Isaac Colquhoun. Despite help from residents, the fire was not brought under control until 12.50 p.m., by which time many of the internal mechanisms had already been destroyed.

THE FIRE CAUSED half of the 100-strong workforce to be laid off indefinitely. A police report into how the fire was started concluded that the fire was believed to have broken out in the drying room due to a lighted stove. However, the manager, Mr L.F. Wastell, declared this statement to be 'rubbish', and added that 'no stove is kept in the room'. Local builders, Messrs Walters & Johns, started to construct the new buildings within days, but it was the damage to the internal apparatus and machinery that prevented employees from returning to work. The works closed in the 1980s under the ownership of Berk Spencer Acids Ltd and Steetley Chemicals Ltd. The site was cleared and Babylon Construction advertised two- and three-bedroomed houses for sale under the proposed name of Samantha Court. The name changed, and Llys Dol was built on the site of the chemical works with no trace of the history of this site, other than the road name, Chemical Road. Llys Dol itself, which translates as Meadow Court, could be referring to the Dingle Farm behind the houses.

CWMRHYDYCEIRW ROAD

THIS IS THE main road that leads from Heol Maes Eglwys through to Chemical Road crossing a boundary from Cwmrhydyceirw to Morriston within seconds. This area had a much cleaner air to breathe than in Morriston, where pollution from the many industries meant smoke-filled skies, and, if the wind changed direction, ruined washing days. The children of Cwmrhydyceirw needed a school of their own because until this happened, the parents of children living here had to send them to Pentrepoeth schools via uneven roads and in all weather conditions. All was about to change when the village had its own cottage school established in the schoolroom of Tabernacle Chapel, just out of shot on the right of the old photograph.

ONE HUNDRED YEARS ago, the number of houses that were situated within
Cwmrhydyceirw was about 120, but they lacked an up-to-date water supply despite the
area flooding profusely. Motions were in place for changes and despite the majority of
people in favour of modernising the water supply, as is often the case, there were a few
that were against it. The hub of Cwmrhydyceirw today is the post office (seen on the left
of both images), which has been in the village for over eighty years. No other part of
Morriston has caused as much outrage and controversy as the Cwmrhydyceirw quarry.
In May 1970, a chunk of rock narrowly missed 16-month-old Sian Gowland as she
played in the garden of her home in Maesygwernen Road, and in June 1975, boulders and
rocks smashed through the windows and roofs at Enfield Close, narrowly missing toddler
Gareth Griffiths. Two hundred people attended a public meeting to apply for a High Court
injunction to stop the blasting of rock at the site, but a handful of the seventy people
employed at the site voted against the decision, saying that it would prove disastrous for
the men and their families. In later years, it became a landfill site.

DANBERT HALL/
DUNBAR HOUSE

A HOUSE OF great distinction; especially at this location as it was built 150 years after the construction of the original grid layout of streets by William Edwards. Danbert Hall, situated on the corner of Lower Morfydd Street and Glantawe Street, is very striking in both photographs, and both images are sad reminders of its splendour. The most recent photograph shows how it has been left to decay since it ceased being the Morriston Employment Exchange. The house was built as the final home of Daniel Edwards, whose name has featured a lot in this book due to the great influence he had on the area.

However, Edwards' died in 1915 at Bedford House whilst Danbert Hall was still under construction. Ironically, the builder later went bankrupt and it remained without a roof for a few more years after Edwards' death.

RECORDS SHOW THAT in 1923, Danbert Hall was the registered office of the Dyffryn Works Ltd, which was founded by Daniel Edwards fifty years prior. Later the residence was renamed Dunbar House when it became the Employment Exchange, where at times queues of people would surround the exterior walls to 'sign on'. By 1980, the Exchange was transferred to new premises at Woodfield Street under the new name of Morriston Job Centre. In 1993, the building was given Grade II listed status by Cadw, which stated at the time that the house was a well-presented example of a large Victorian town house rare to Morriston. Cadw is a body of the Welsh government with the mission to conserve the country's heritage and sustain the distinctive character of Wales. Over recent years, the house has been left abandoned, caught fire numerous times and has been partially destroyed. At present the building and land is owned separately by people living outside the area and there are calls for its demolition.

DAVID MICHAEL JEWELLERS

DAVID MICHAEL WAS a partnership founded in
1974 between David Hopkins and his brother-in-law
Michael Price. The first shop opened in Gwydr Square,
Uplands, followed four weeks later by its Morriston
branch at No. 129 Woodfield Street, later moving to
No. 114 Woodfield Street. David Hopkins had been a
manager at Tom Evans based in Swansea City Centre and
Michael Price had trained to become a goldsmith. After a
successful period in Morriston and Uplands, David and
Michael decided to expand their business into the city,
acquiring premises on High Street and at the Quadrant
Swansea, where they stayed until moving to premises at
Whitewalls in Swansea. They expanded further in 1986
when they opened at Queen Street in Neath.

After an amicable end to their partnership, Michael resided over the High Street store, which closed when he retired from the jewellery trade. David continues to work at the shop in Neath and his wife, Janice, ran the Morriston shop until her retirement when the running of the shop was passed to grandson Kyle Hopkins. The business is now in its fortieth year.

THE OLDER IMAGE was taken by staff member Patricia Jenkins during Christmas 1994. From left to right: Jean Williams, Pauline Stock, Janice Hopkins, Margaret Jones and Betty Haynes.

Betty was well known in Morriston having worked at David Michael Jewellers for many years. Sadly, she passed away in November 2012.

The more modern photograph of staff at David Michael Jewellers was taken in February 2013. From left to right: Caroline Harris, Kyle Hopkins (Manager), Janice Hopkins (Proprietor) and Pauline Stock.

FIRE STATION

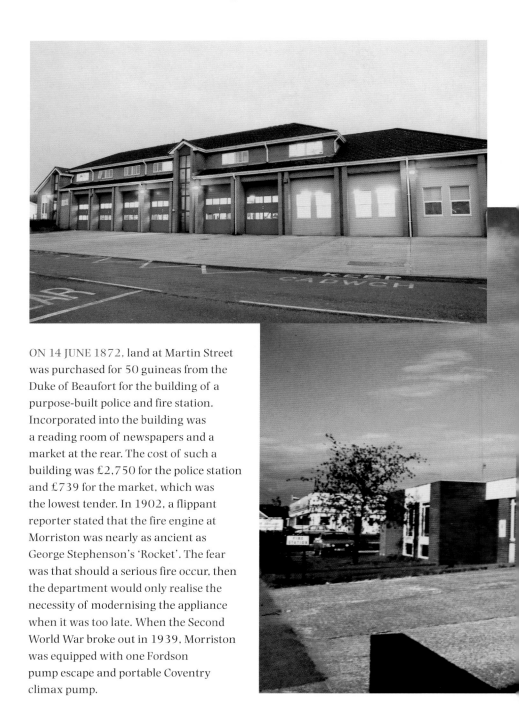

ON 14 JUNE 1872, land at Martin Street was purchased for 50 guineas from the Duke of Beaufort for the building of a purpose-built police and fire station. Incorporated into the building was a reading room of newspapers and a market at the rear. The cost of such a building was £2,750 for the police station and £739 for the market, which was the lowest tender. In 1902, a flippant reporter stated that the fire engine at Morriston was nearly as ancient as George Stephenson's 'Rocket'. The fear was that should a serious fire occur, then the department would only realise the necessity of modernising the appliance when it was too late. When the Second World War broke out in 1939, Morriston was equipped with one Fordson pump escape and portable Coventry climax pump.

THE OLDER PHOTO shows the first purpose-built fire station with a three-bay appliance room in Sway Road. It was opened on 14 March 1969 by the Mayor of Swansea, Councillor David Jenkins. West Glamorgan County Fire Service Headquarters Complex was officially opened on 26 February 1992, but is now sadly closed and up for sale. West Glamorgan Fire Service was formed taking under its wing the former Central, West Cross and Morriston stations. In 1988, the three-bay station was demolished and two years later, the impressive nine-bay Mid and West Wales Fire Safety and Training Headquarters was built and opened on the site. In 2012, Morriston was fighting plans to keep all of its fire engines when plans were revealed to exchange a fire engine for a rural response pump. A rural response pump would take Morriston's progress back to the early 1900s; especially when one considers that there is a major hospital and busy motorway (M4) on the doorstep of the town. Since 2012, the station has shared its facilities with the Welsh Ambulance Service Trust where one ambulance and crew is located.

GEM AUTO CENTRE

ALTHOUGH THIS SITE can be dated back to a mission hall used as temporary accommodation while its members were waiting for St David's Church to be built, the building in this pair of photographs will be remembered by older Morristonians as the Gem Cinema from the 1920s until 1958. Its first use was as the Niagra Skating Rink but picture houses were all the rage just before the advent of the First World War. In July 1913, the Amman Alpha Cinema Ltd was registered, and went on to establish numerous picture houses around South Wales, which included Morriston in March 1914. The Alpha Cinema (in competition to its rival and more upmarket Picturedrome at Woodfield Street) attracted its customers in its opening weeks by showing Pathé colour film. The Alpha in Morriston also housed a benefit concert in aid of John Williams, a tinman from the Beaufort Works who had been ill for a long period and the money raised helped him out of poverty. The benefit system had not been established at that time.

DESPITE THE INITIAL hype over the launch of the Alpha, by July it had closed. The manager, Mr Frank Denvers, feeling responsible over the failure of the cinema, was found dead in his office at the cinema by police after an officer passing by the front doors smelt gas. It was said that the gas was so strong that the use of an ordinary lamp would have had a disastrous effect on that part of Morriston. Years later, the building opened as the Gem Cinema. Unlike its rival, which was the Regal in Woodfield Street, the Gem Cinema did not have an upstairs. It was plain and square and could sit a maximum of 500 people. On Mondays and Fridays, you could go to the Regal, then to the Gem on Tuesdays and Thursdays. These cinemas brought an escape from the everyday world of the tinplate works. Although, one major flaw at the Gem was that anyone sitting in the front rows would suffer from a stiff neck after the film. If you knew someone working there, you could get in without having to pay. The Gem closed in the late 1950s, but even today, it is a landmark building as Gem Autocentre.

GLANTAWE STREET

GLANTAWE STREET GIVES us a glimpse of what Woodfield Street would have looked like without its many shops and the famous Tabernacle Chapel. The street runs parallel with Woodfield Street from which many of the original grid layout streets are attached. The images look towards Clase Road, but the first obvious difference is that more cars park on Glantawe Street now than in 1987 (when the older photograph was taken) with allocated residents' parking outside the houses. The second change to have affected this part of the street is the ten one-bedroom flats called Ty Fforest that were built in 2002 on the site of the Cyril Cooke warehouse that was for many years home to Wesleyan Methodist Church.

WESLEYAN METHODIST CHURCH was licensed for marriages on 4 April 1940, but closed in January 1963. In 1970, Mr Ernest Jones who had lived at No. 18 Glantawe Street for the past forty-five years reflected that during those years, the character of the street had been completely altered by redevelopment. Houses have been replaced by small garages and many of the newly constructed shops on Woodfield Street have their loading bays in Glantawe Street. Mr D. Clifford Jones of No. 102 Glantawe Street said that his home had been devalued due to the proximity of a supermarket, a licensed club and a taxi firm. The street saw its second accident in a twenty-four-hour period during the afternoon of 16 June 1973 when two cars collided. A 2-year-old girl received a broken leg on the previous night when she was struck by a car near to her home.

GROVE PLACE CHAPEL, CLYDACH ROAD

SITUATED ON CLYDACH ROAD, this former church was owned by the Forward Movement Presbyterian Church of Wales, which was a sister church to its large venue in Woodfield Street that was once the Morriston Opera Hall. Grove Place Church had many foundation stones laid on 6 December 1913 by distinguished people such as Thomas J. Williams of Maesygwernen Hall and Estate (which later became Morriston Hospital), and Councillor David Matthews who was Mayor of Swansea in 1909, and 1910–11 and lived at Llwyneyr House on Clasemont Road. The hall was opened by the Revd J.M. Jones of Cardiff who was the superintendent of the Forward Movement.

THE YEAR 1926 saw the schoolroom being constructed on the left of the main building
and many tablets were unveiled in the wall. They included the headmistress of Pentrepoeth
Infants School, Miss Jane Donne; the wife of Mr Emrys Jones of Barclays Bank in
Woodfield Street; Mr and Mrs Heslop, business people from Woodfield Street; Doctors Gabe
and Kemp and Sister Alison Jones who was an integral part of the history of Grove Place.
Sister Alison was a greatly admired minister of Grove Place from 1916 until she died on
30 April 1960. Today the building has been converted into five three-bedroom dwellings,
designed by ADI Interior Design. Trinity Chapel, as it was sometimes referred to, is now
simply called Grove Place of No. 160 Clydach Road.

HOREB CHAPEL,
HOREB ROAD

HOREB CHAPEL WAS originally built in 1842. The older image (taken in 1986) shows the rebuild of 1869 by the well-known chapel architect, John Humphrey who also designed Tabernacle, Martin Street School and Morriston Primary. Horeb was restored in 1929 by changing the entrance to Horeb Road, prior to that, entrance was gained at the rear of the chapel. In the early 1900s, the Horeb Congregational Choir would enter the National Eisteddfod choir competitions against William Penfro Rowlands' Morriston Choir, which, of course, meant that they never won. William composed the hymn tune 'Blaenwern' in 1905. Music played a very important role in all of the churches and chapels in Morriston, none more so than in Horeb. In 1956, their children's choir performed *Snow White and the Seven Dwarfs* in the schoolroom under the main chapel. However, the dwindling congregation at Horeb had a devastating effect on the future of the building.

THE CHAPEL WAS closed in 1987 and sold to a developer who submitted plans to Swansea City Council requesting permission to adapt the building into twenty-two one-bedroom flats and a caretaker's flat. There was concern that the architectural value of the building would be severely damaged, so delays were put in place to discuss the matter with the developer. While discussions took place over a period of a year or more, the structure of the building deteriorated quickly, and when the country suffered hurricane weather conditions in early February 1990, the building became unsafe. The striking architectural feature, which was the rear wall facing Woodfield Street, had to be demolished with the rest of the building. Some gravestones were damaged during the demolition process, which caused a lot of anger and upset for relatives of loved ones buried there. The gravestones that survived are now lying flat at the back of the new Ty Horeb complex that was built on the site of this historic chapel.

HUNT'S/
SUN LOUNGE

THE OLDER PHOTOGRAPH shows the inside of the bakery of a
well-known Morriston business that attracted customers mainly
with their hot pies, from the 1930s until the late 1970s. William
Hunt was born in Swindon around 1886. He was a master baker
and married Georgina Thomas at Llanelli in 1909. They started
their business at Woodfield Street, living above No. 53 and baking
below Nos 52–54. They had five children; the two sons, Kenneth
and Norman, were master bakers producing wedding cakes of
the highest standard. William Hunt died on 29 September 1936.
In his will, he left £5,558 11s 4d to his wife, who was a presence
in the shop until her death at the age of 102 in 1977. She was
known to sit by the ornate till that still sprung up pre-decimal
prices. After her death, the business was sold and the whole
building was bought by Charles Sayers, who was running
Martins' Glassware in part of the building.

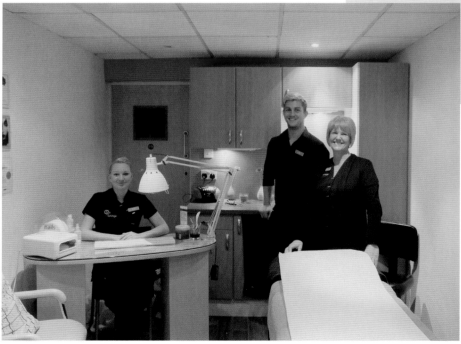

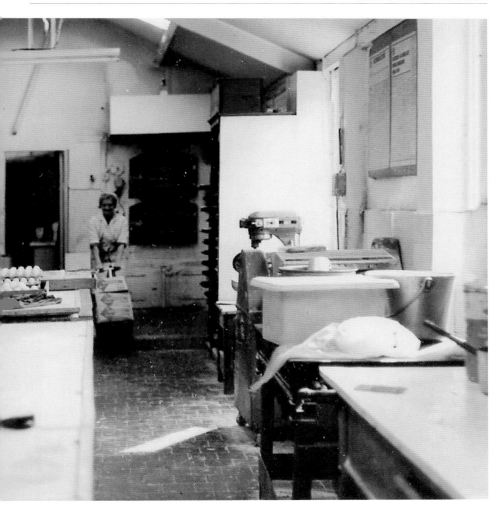

SAYERS STAYED UNTIL 1993 when the building was bought and extensively altered by Morriston Jobcentre, who remained in the premises for thirteen years, using the former bakery as a storage area. They cleaned the building externally and refurbished the interior to a high quality. After the Jobcentre vacated the building, it remained unoccupied until the bakery and other rooms became the home of The Sun Lounge Beauty & Tanning Centre in March 2009. Keeping the family tradition alive once more is the owner, Bonnie Fisher, with her children Alex (manager) and Sarah (beauty therapist) pictured in the more modern photograph in one of their therapy rooms. The business opened in 2000.

MORRISTON LIBRARY

A RARE PHOTO to mark the retirement of librarian Mrs J.M. Evans (right), with colleague Lynne Powell. The older image affords a view of how the library once looked; complete with a reading room for daily newspapers and the ticket machines that allowed librarians to find out which books had been taken out and which ones were overdue. From 1873–77, the only resources available to the Morriston population was a reading room with weekly newspapers – not much to educate and stimulate. On 9 November 1877, a collection of books was added by way of voluntary contributions, therefore, it was called a library, but it shared little resemblance to what we traditionally call a library. In 1903, there was public outcry that Morriston did not have its own branch library. Sharing the premises with the police station in Martin Street meant that Morristonians felt neglected, the population

wanted to learn and to borrow books but limited space meant limited reading matter. It took another sixty years for changes to happen!

THE CURRENT MORRISTON Library was officially opened on Tuesday, 10 April 1962 by Councillor T.R. Davies, a representative of the ward and chairman of the Libraries' Committee. The building at Treharne Road was designed by Mr H.T. Wykes and constructed by Rees & Kirby Ltd of Morriston, and was built at a cost of £20,000, serving the community very well over the years. Currently, the library has many facilities that could only have been dreamt about years ago; computers with free internet access replace the newspapers, a reading section for children and teenagers, and reading matter to appeal to all ages. It is attracting more than 400–500 people per day through its door. The librarians no longer 'shush' you for talking. The library's manager Pat Perkins and library assistant Debra Young (seen in the more modern photograph, left and right respectively) are approachable and helpful. A lot has changed since the 1986 photograph and the library celebrated its fiftieth anniversary in 2012 – the future looks promising. In April 2013, the Welsh Assembly Government promised £218,000 for a much-needed makeover to help boost literacy levels in the area. The library closed in 2013 to make these changes.

MARTIN STREET

LOOKING UP MARTIN STREET in 1910 towards
St John's Church (in the middle of the road),
and in the distance is the tower of Tabernacle
Chapel. On the left is the Cambrian Arms public
house that can be dated back to 1873 when the
landlord was George Jenkins. For many years,
Mr Frederick Thissen was the licensee after
inheriting the interest in the publican trade from
his father Leonard, who ran the Duke Arms.
Frederick died at just 51 years of age; he and
his family are buried at Bethel Cemetery at
Llangyfelach. Daniel and Louisa Rewbridge were
the proprietors of the Cambrian Arms in the
1940s. Today, the building has been converted
from a house into flats.

THE BUILDING ON the right of both images opened
in 1875 as Morriston's second police station,
replacing the old station at Neath Road, the cells
of which were added in 1856. The land for the

police station in Martin Street was acquired from the Duke of Beaufort for 50 guineas. It was built by Thomas White for £2,750, with an additional £739 for a market at the rear of the building. There was also a county police station at No. 50 Clydach Road where officers would live on the premises. The Martin Street police station was controlled in 1887 by Inspector Henry Williams and assisted by Sergeant John Bowden and Police Constable Henry Morris. Records show that in 1900 the Morriston police force consisted of Inspector Benjamin Eynon of No. 52 Market Street, PC Cornelius John of No. 13 Sydney Crescent in Banwell Street and PC Thomas Tanner of No. 25 Banwell Street, all living in close proximity of the station. The building was also used as a fire station and library. In recent years, the building was converted into accommodation. The shop on the right of the older photograph was the first location for Harry's Stores, which later moved to Clase Road. The Harrys were a big family running grocery stores and licensed premises in the 1850s. Opposite Harry's Stores, pictured here was Martin Street Post Office, said to be the first post office in Morriston with postmaster Mr Thomas Harry! It later became a newsagent and is now Just Jenny's Florist.

MARTIN STREET BOYS' SCHOOL

WHEN MARTIN STREET Boys' School opened in 1868, it shared many of its facilities with the community of Morriston and was often the venue of Morriston concerts. Many of the concerts were held in connection with its sister school, Neath Road (now Morriston Primary School), which also opened in 1868. In the summer of 1903, the central hall of Martin Street School was redecorated for a concert to bid farewell to a young Martin Street grocer, Mr Frank Davies, who was leaving for Cape Town at a time when a lot of residents were leaving for this destination. Many smartly dressed young women and men were at this concert where Davies was presented with a gold watch supplied by renowned Morriston jeweller, Mr Walter Tracey of Woodfield Street. Dr Charles Kemp stood up to

speak and to wish Mr Davies a safe trip and a happy life in South Africa. The audience sung 'For He's a Jolly Good Fellow' and after a few songs and recitals from various local personalities, including a police constable, the concert was ended with rendition of 'Auld Lang Syne' and the attendees joining hands.

IT WAS PROPOSED in 1972 to alter the catchment areas of both Pentrepoeth Junior Girls and Martin Street Junior Boys, and to allow opposite sexes into each school, but this proposal fell by the wayside. Martin Street eventually fell into disrepair and it closed in 1988, and transferred to Pentrepoeth Junior Girls' School. The last headmaster of Martin Street, Mr David Gimblett, became the first headteacher at the new Pentrepoeth Junior School. The Martin Street building was used temporarily by Graig Infants when their building was being renovated, but, in 1991, the bulldozers moved in and the entire site was demolished. St Martin's Court Care Home (now owned by HC-One) was built on the site of the school and the schoolyard. It contains sixty-eight bedrooms offering nursing, residential and respite care.

MORFYDD STREET

THE SMALL COTTAGE pictured in both photographs is on Upper Morfydd Street. It is the oldest surviving house in Morriston. It is possible that it is older than any other building in the town, but it has also been said that it was built around the same time as Morriston's first place of worship, Libanus in Market Street (1782). It is believed that this is how all of the houses in Morris Town looked when John Morris' engineer and architect the Revd William Edwards laid out the original town. Copperworkers and colliers would build their cottages to the plans set out by Edwards, to create a uniform appearance. Later on, the houses were joined into terraces and replaced leaving just this house and a slightly later dwelling in Woodfield Street, which also exists today at No. 91a (opposite Wilkinson) although it has been altered so much that it no longer resembles a cottage.

THE OLDER PHOTOGRAPH was taken in 1983 and shows the house in a disused state, which was unusual at the time, because it was a period when hardly anything in Morriston was disused, abandoned or unloved. There was a great deal of speculation about the future of the cottage at this point and many wondered if a buyer could be found in its state of disrepair. Thankfully, it was purchased and renovated to a high standard. The cottage is a superb example of the type of houses one would have lived in during the 1780s. Originally, the house was known as No. 14 Edward Street and although the street name changed to Morfydd Street around 1909, the house numbers were altered later, therefore making this property No. 35 Morfydd Street.

MORRISTON COMPREHENSIVE SCHOOL

MONDAY, 17 MAY 1971 saw a plaque unveiled that officially opened the new Morriston Senior Comprehensive School that was built by Gee, Walker & Slater (the junior comprehensive was at Llansamlet).

The mayor's chaplain, the Revd Peter Williams, performed a service of dedication witnessed by civil dignitaries, the staff of twenty-five, the children and the school's first headteacher, Mr T.H. Chandler. The ceremony in the school hall ended with the Welsh national anthem being sung, followed by 'God Save the Queen'. On the staff roll that day was Mr Ken Harries, a former PE teacher at Pentrepoeth Boys' School. He was instrumental in arranging a yearly Eisteddfod on St David's Day, something he achieved

with infectious enthusiasm. His teaching manner meant that the children and staff loved him dearly and were devastated to learn of his incurable illness and his sad passing in 1989. A memorial chair carved by woodwork teacher Mr Clatworthy is still present at the school.

THE SCHOOL SITE today has changed greatly, with Morriston Leisure Centre attached and new state-of-the-art buildings replacing the old. The future of the school is evident from the artistic plans that have been printed. Among ongoing improvements a new teaching block (featured in the modern photo) was opened on 20 June 2008, and a learning resource centre and the 'Hub' are to replace A and B Block: these block names are indelibly etched on ex-pupils' minds from the old Morriston Senior Comprehensive School.

OLD BRIDGE

THE AREA OF Old Bridge in Morriston encompassed Nixon Terrace, Bush Road, Dyffryn Terrace and Williams Row. Williams Row were a pair of semi-detached cottages that had been converted from an old coach-house dating back to the early 1700s and situated off a lane alongside the gospel hall, which can be seen in the older photograph taken in 1977. As you walked down Nixon Terrace, you would have seen the grey-painted wooden structure standing alone, but with its door open wide and a warm welcome to anyone who went inside. Originally, there was a row of similar houses and the gospel hall started when one family who lived there began holding services in their front room. The houses were owned by the Forest & Worcester Tinplate Works (now the site of Asda) and when it was decided in 1905 to demolish the row, the end house was reprieved and converted into a chapel. The rent was a mere 1s (5p) per year and in later years it was rent free.

THE ORIGINAL HOUSE consisted of two rooms downstairs and two rooms upstairs, but the whole interior was removed to make one open room allowing 120 people to pack into the small hall where they would hear Mrs Olive Morris play the organ and various lay preachers stand on the pulpit, booked by the chapel superintendent, Mr Tommy Hone. In 1977, Old Bridge Gospel Hall was to be demolished to make way for the Morriston bypass, but the bulldozers struggled to pull it down! They finally managed the job and a small consolation was achieved when the gospel hall moved into the vacant Salem Methodist Chapel, used at one time by Bethania Sunday school at Nixon Terrace just a stone's-throw away from the original site. However, as the faithful congregation grew too small to justify its existence, the Old Bridge Gospel Hall ceased worship.

OPERA
HOUSE

THE BUILDING IN between the shops shown
in the older photograph was built in the 1890s
as the Morriston Public Hall. It was built by a
company of Morriston workmen and tradesmen
who failed to make money for its shareholders.
It was then bought by Mr Oakley Walters
(of Walters & John, builders) who purchased it
for £1,800. In 1897, the building became known
as the Morriston Opera House and had one of the
largest stages in Wales with a seating capacity
of over 1,000. A 23-year-old actor called Alfred
Denville was appointed manager two years
later; he started the first professional repertory
company in the country, here at this building in
Woodfield Street.

ONE OF ALFRED'S plays at the Opera House on 22 August 1902 was entitled
For the Colours, featuring four black Zulu actors. After the performance, one of the actors
crossed the street and chatted to a local woman. An inebriated Morriston man happened
to be passing and made an indecent remark about the actor. The taunts continued and
the actor threw the local man across the street. A fight ensued in the front of the theatre
doors as the actor was supported by his fellow cast members and their spears which had
been used as props for the production. Many people were hurt, including the landlord of
the Welcome public house. The hall was purchased in 1973 by Tesco, who demolished it to
extend their store.

PARK

TEN TO FIFTEEN years before Morriston Park was opened, the need for an open space high above the smoky, industrial town was eagerly anticipated, but often thwarted as it was either not taken seriously or the landowners failed to go through with the plan. One setback that Morriston faced just as they thought their requests had been answered was learning that Kilvrough Lady of the Manor, Louisa Jane Lyons, wouldn't grant a piece of land for the purpose of a park, but would continue charging rent on the houses and businesses on land at Pentrepoeth and other parts of Morriston. Residents had started to wonder if their dream of a park would ever come true or whether they would still be challenging landowners and arguing their cause for another fifteen years.

Land was eventually purchased and a little pressure on Lady Lyons meant that she felt obliged to give the Pleasant Street entrance free of charge to a brand new Morriston Park. Therefore, on a Saturday morning in the pouring rain, the park was eventually opened

in June 1912 (even then they had wet summers!).
Councillor David Matthews was presented with a
gold key and he then declared Morriston Park open.
The area was 42 acres and it cost £7,092 to lay out
with the annual expenditure estimated to be at £550.
It was designed by 40-year-old Mr Daniel Bliss, a park
superintendent from Sketty. Morriston Baths opened
on Saturday, 12 July 1913 by the Mayor of Swansea,
Councillor David Williams. It was 75ft by 35ft and 3ft
in the shallow end rising to 6ft in the deep end, with
the only problem being the coldness of the water as
is was sourced from a nearby stream. Heating was
promised providing it was well patronised by the people
of Morriston. It is pictured on the left of the older
photograph, taken in 1973 during a cricket match.

TODAY, THE SITE of the baths is occupied by a
BMX track. The majority of Morristonians will say
that the baths are the most missed activity at the park
today. Sadly, in June 2012, the park failed to celebrate its
100th anniversary due to weather and park conditions.
It is important for the current residents of the town to
honour the legacy of those that fought for the park by its
continued use.

PENTREMALWED ROAD

THE MOST STRIKING house in the older image (taken in 1986) is Pentremalwed House, which was built around the 1850s. It was not until its demolition in January 2012 that anyone realised that the house was built of pole stone, as everyone remembered it with its white façade. Records show that the house was often occupied by insurance agents and their families. In 1911–14, Leonard Heslop lived in the house with his family. During the Second World War, the house proved too big for owner Blodwen Reed, so she rented out rooms to Emlyn and Hilda Davies, and Jonah and Dorothy Phillips. In the 1950s, the new owners were Walter and Margaret Mead with their six children.

(The author is proud to say that he lived at Pentremalwed House with his parents, Joan and Denzil Scoville.) More recently, after some time as bedsits, the house was empty and the fire brigade was often called to a fire at the house. The building started to deteriorate leading to parts being demolished by new owners in January 2012, with a view to rebuilding and converting it into two separate houses. The retaining garden wall of red Graig bricks was demolished on 14 February 2013 and replaced by a wall using the new pole stone as used on the house.

AS CAN BE seen from the older image, the road is nothing like its former self. The houses were demolished between 1986–89 due to a landslip that not only affected this part of Pentremalwed Road, but also parts of Plas-y-Coed and Graig Road, a row of terraced houses on the banks of Clyndu Street and a house at the entrance to Bath Villas. This does not seem to have been anything new for the area, because in November 1888 a surveyor reported that Pentremalwed Road was in a dangerous state and the Swansea Health Board decided to bring this fact to the attention of the owners. The contrast between then and now regarding this road shows that the area has largely gone uncared for since the demolition of the houses.

PENTREPOETH DINING HALL

IN 1992, THIS site was occupied by the Pentrepoeth Dining Hall and Kitchens, a place that would make all of the dinners for the schools in the area and then distribute them in metal boxes. The older photograph was taken from Waun Road and captured again in the more modern image twenty years later. It shows how much the site has changed. Gwalia Housing Group started building work on the site in February 1995 and when finished the complex was called Cwrt Ifor Simms, after the Pentrepoeth schoolteacher and gifted musician, Ivor Sims, who founded the Morriston Orpheus Choir and the Pentrepoeth

Boys Choir. Ivor Evan Sims (1896–1961) was born at Llansamlet, the fourth child of seven to Evan Evan Sims (a general printer) and Hannah Sims.

THE SIMS FAMILY lived No. 12 Glantawe Street surrounded by printing machinery where, at just 6 years old, Ivor Sims was found reading anthem proofs that had been printed by his father. He was educated at Dynevor School and Kings College, London where he read music and maths. In 1928, after teaching at Waun Wen, he took up a position at Pentrepoeth Senior Boys' School in Morriston where he founded the school choir called Pentrepoeth Boys' Choir and became organist at St David's Church, Morriston. Nazareth Chapel's Gwalia Choir changed its name to Morriston United Choir where Ivor acted as accompanist, but a split within the choir over its choice of music led some members to want to form a choir with Ivor Sims as their leader. On 23 April 1935, the now world-famous Morriston Orpheus Male Voice Choir was formed at Wesleyan Methodist Church vestry on Glantawe Street. Ivor Evan Sims passed away at Morriston Hospital on 6 April 1961 just before he was to retire as headmaster of Hafod Secondary Mixed School. He was just 64 years of age. A plaque in his memory can be seen on the outside wall of Morriston Library.

PENTREPOETH ROAD

ONE OF THE oldest roads that has seen much of Morriston's history over the years is Pentrepoeth Road. It has seen major road alterations, road crashes, cars and lorries that have burst into flames, and was the location of one of Morriston's largest general practice surgeries. Just the mere task of lighting up a main road like this at the turn of the twentieth century caused great complications. The Corporation decided that gas lamps were needed at Pentrepoeth Hill because trying to negotiate it in complete darkness was dangerous for both pedestrians and horse-drawn vehicles. The Corporation invested in gas lamps for this road (also on Bath Road). It was more than a year later, in October 1902, when they finally shone.

MORRISTON, INCLUDING PENTREPOETH
Road was given a substantial redevelopment
in 1930–32. One side of the road was stripped
of its thatched cottages to make way for a
wider road allowing for the new motor cars
that had started appearing. Even thirty years
after the improvements, drivers were still urged
to observe signs warning them to slow their
speed when travelling down Pentrepoeth Hill
as 15-ton loaded lorries could not stop in time;
the level of traffic was helped by the construction
of the M4 bypass. The worst crash to affect
the residents of Pentrepoeth Road was on
12 August 1971, when three people were injured
in an accident that saw a 10-ton lorry crash
into the middle of the hill where it then burst
into flames. The driver was thrown through the
windscreen on impact. The Morriston bypass
could not come quickly enough.

Pentrepoeth House, on the right just out
of view in both images, was accommodation
for many surgeons and general practitioners
throughout the years. Dr Henry Davies
(surgeon) was the first person to live in the
house in 1869. The last GP to practise there was
Dr Clifford Jones.

PHILADELPHIA CHAPEL

PICTURED IN THE older photograph in 1983 is Philadelphia Calvinistic Methodist Chapel, which opened in 1802, was enlarged in 1812 and was rebuilt in 1829; and is a Grade II listed building. Philadelphia was registered for marriages on 22 October 1862. Philadelphia means 'brotherly love'; although the reason Philadelphia Chapel exists is that some members of Libanus did not like the minister that was appointed, so they resigned their membership and formed a Methodist church. History repeated itself in 1878 when some of Philadelphia's members formed a new chapel called Bethania in Woodfield Street.

THE 1829 REBUILD saw the chapel expanded to accommodate over 700 members, with an additional chapel house attached on the end, which was on the corner of

Morris Street. The Revd Thomas Levi caused a stir when he protested against the holding of the Llangyfelach fair on a Sunday; he was victorious when the Markets and Fairs Act of 1847 was passed preventing them from opening on the Sabbath. The chapel was remodelled inside and out in 1930 by Thomas & Jones, builders of Morriston. Central heating by a coal-fired boiler was installed at a cost of £124. The numbers attending in the latter part of the twentieth century could not afford to keep the chapel going and it struggled to celebrate its 200th anniversary in 2002; the end was definitely in sight when only one evening service per Sunday proved too much for some of the elderly members. The chapel consequently closed and the building's future looked uncertain, until Morriston-based company, Advanced Heating Wales Ltd bought the building and renovated it to a very high standard, converting it into flats and an office. The renovation was completed in 2011, and the building is as beautiful inside as it appears on the outside, which can be seen in the modern photograph.

RED LION PUBLIC HOUSE

THOUGH DRAMATICALLY ALTERED since early 2011 when the Red Lion was bought by national pub chain, Wetherspoons, it has always remained at the core of Morristonians throughout the years, never more so than now. The interior of the Wetherspoons-owned Red Lion contains many framed images from the author's Morriston archive collection, along with some lovely paintings of Morriston and a giant Monkey Puzzle Tree. Records of the Red Lion go back to 1849 when Mr D. Davies was the licensee of the then thatched cottage Red Lion. Over the years, the history records show that families have bequeathed the public house throughout their generations; for over forty years, John Charles Jones was the licensee who then passed it on to his son,

John Samuel Jones. Then from 1938 until the 1970s, the Red Lion was run by the Davies family who consisted of John, Maggie, Brian and Dorothy.

FOR A GOOD many years, Brian Jones was the proprietor; he built a large function room at the rear of the premises. The pub played host to many evenings of after-concert drinking from the Morriston Orpheus and Morriston Ladies choirs. The pub has a relaxing atmostphere and is an ideal place for social gatherings. As with many of Britain's towns and cities, Morriston has seen a number of pub closures over the last few years. Those pubs that have closed their doors include The Bevans Arms, Crown Inn, Cross Inn, Lamb & Flag, Plough Inn, and the Bird in Hand called 'last orders' on Friday, 5 April 2013; Lynne Davies was at the helm for over thirty years, and many of those were with her late husband, Peter. It was an emotional night – an end of an era. As for the Wetherspoons' Red Lion, a beer garden was opened in the spring of 2013, making this venue one of the best in Swansea for a quiet chat surrounded by everything that is Morriston.

ST JOHN'S CHURCH (IN THE MIDDLE OF THE ROAD)

THIS CHURCH IS the focal point of Morriston; named after John Morris, the original St John's Church was consecrated on 21 November 1789 and was built with wood. What stands today was built at a cost of £1,400 and opened on 10 July 1862. The tower was added in 1871. The ancient landmark was able to celebrate its 200th anniversary in 1989 but a mere ten years later, the Church of Wales sold the building to a private owner. In 1902, evergreens had been placed around the church by a member of the congregation with the thought that the plants would enhance the quaintness of such an important building in Morriston. The bell tower held six bells that were installed in

1879 and to herald in the New Year at the turn of the twentieth century, the bells would be rung and heard throughout Morriston. In 1902, they rang a muffled peal marking the funeral of Queen Victoria. Sadly, the bells had to be removed in 1953 due to a severe case of dry rot and they were never put back. They were sold in 1977.

IN 1961, THE vicar of St John's Church asked Mr John Mitchell to construct a cross which could be lit up at night on a temporary basis and hung from the top of the tower of the church. This cross became a landmark in itself. During a severe gale in 1971, the cross was damaged and it became apparent to the Church that it was important to the community. The cross was replaced and it stayed on the top of the tower until the mid- to late 1980s and its remains can still be seen at the top of the tower today. The church, known as 'the church in the middle of the road', is a truly historic site and one that must be preserved for future generations to come.

STRAWBERRY PLACE SURGERY

IN JUST TEN years, the difference is truly startling. The purchase of houses at Strawberry Place to extend the old surgery and to create the new practice, with adjoining chemist, took place in 2006–07. The surgery at No. 5 Strawberry Place, at a house called Glyn Mefus, commenced around the early 1930s, run by a grocer's son named John Cyril Edwards-Jones (b. 1900). Edwards-Jones grew up at Crown Stores at Gorseinon's High Street, with his two brothers and many staff who helped his father with the business. On 5 January 1925,

while living with his parents in Gorseinon as a medical student, John changed his name by deed poll from John Cyril Jones, taking on his mother's maiden name as well, to be known as John Cyril Edwards-Jones. He qualified in 1928. Dr Cyril, as most called him, was well known in Morriston and had a reputation for not charging those suffering financial hardship. He passed away in 1964; his wife, Nest, died at her daughter's home in Westminster, London in the mid-1980s. Their daughter, Diana Edwards-Jones, was a very successful TV director who started her career on ITN's *News at Ten*.

IN AROUND 1949, Dr Cyril was joined by RAF Officer, Dr Peter Grant Jagger who was born in 1921 in Neath (Grant was his mother Lillian's maiden name having married George Jagger in Port Talbot in 1921). Peter Grant Jagger's grandfather was a doctor in Manchester. Peter married Brenda Phillips in Cardiff in 1945 and had two children: Robert Grant Jagger born in 1947 at Cardiff and Catherine Grant Jagger born in Swansea in 1950. Dr Peter Jagger passed away in 1982, just eighteen months after the death of his wife Brenda in June 1980. Dr June Thomas joined the practice in the 1970s with Dr Roberts and they practised here for many years.

SWAY ROAD PUBLIC CONVENIENCES

THE PUBLIC CONVENIENCES shown in the older photograph were for both men and women, and located at Sway Road (pictured here before they were demolished in 1986). Today, the site is occupied by a brand new building. The only public conveniences that exist today in Morriston are to be found at the top of Woodfield Street, built in the very early 1980s. They are open from 9 a.m. until 5 p.m. and there is an attendant in charge of their upkeep.

Morriston toilets have never been as clean as they are now and, in fact, the only ladies public lavatories were the ones photographed here at Sway Road. The rest, and there were many, were for men and they were often situated either near or next to a public house.

ONE OF THE most talked-about men's urinals was situated on the traffic island of St John's Church. The wrought-iron space without a roof could be looked in on from the top of a double-decker bus and nearly everyone would look to see if anyone was using the toilet, mainly out of curiosity of course. The toilet served the Powells Arms (later called The Champion) and The Bevans Arms. There was a urinal on Glantawe Street, near the cutting for Margam Avenue, frequented by the regulars of the Dillwyn Arms public house opposite. The Dukes Arms had an outside men's urinal that went down steps at the side of the pub and, until recently, the handrail was still visable. There was also a men's urinal next to The Cross Inn on Pentrepoeth Road, which later became part of The Cross Inn itself. Ladies drew the short straw when it came to public conveniences in Morriston, but they were not expected or invited to public houses in the early twentieth century, although they were considered good enough to serve in them! Fortunately, pubs and times have changed.

THOMAS & JONES BUILDERS MERCHANTS

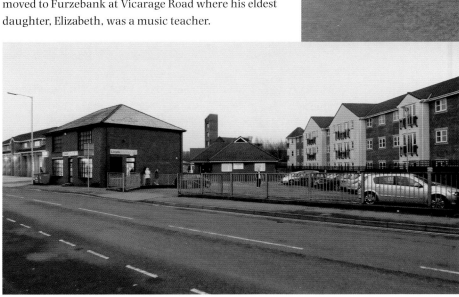

THE IMAGES SHOW what was once the business premises of William Thomas and Eleazer Jones at Sway Yard, photographed in 1986 a year before it was demolished and the same view in 2013. At an extraordinary general meeting held at No. 155 Vicarage Road on 27 March 1987, Thomas & Jones (Morriston) Ltd was voluntarily wound up by the chairman of the company, Thomas Allison, brother to John Allison CBE JP who passed away on 25 May 2012 at the age of 92. Mr William Thomas was born in 1859 at Cwmafan. After marrying Mary Amelia Rott in 1890, the house builder set up home at No. 16 Slate Street and had two children, Elizabeth and Gwendoline. Twenty years later, the family had moved to Furzebank at Vicarage Road where his eldest daughter, Elizabeth, was a music teacher.

WILLIAM'S BUSINESS PARTNER, Eleazer Jones, was born in 1856 at Morriston and was the son of a watchman living at Neath Road, between the Globe Inn and the Dolphin Inn. Eleazer started his working life as a cold roller in the tinplate works, but when he married Eleanor Lewis, in 1890, he moved into his mother-in-law's house at No. 38 Woodfield Street; she was becoming frail and was 83 years of age. Eleazer and Eleanor had three children, and Eleazer died in 1929, aged 73. Lloyds Pharmacy stands on the site of the ironmongers having been built a year after the old site was cleared. On the land once occupied by the builders' yard, New Cross Surgery and car park were built on the site, being officially opened by Dr E.A. Danino on 27 October 1989. Thomas & Jones were funeral directors as well as builders.

TIRCANOL
TINPLATE WORKS

THE TINPLATE INDUSTRY dominated Morriston in the late nineteenth century until the mid-1950s. Anyone old enough to either remember the works in action or the buildings left abandoned will know how many there were. This was the Morriston Midland & Tircanol works back in 1986 prior to the whole site being demolished. In the 1970s, the Morriston Midland Works was operating from this building, but it was nothing compared to the harsh conditions of working here in the 1900s; David Haeney started working here in 1896 at the age of 12, and would work seven days a week (7 a.m. until 4.30 p.m.) earning just 12s per week (60p today). Eventually, he became foreman and was known as 'Gaffer Bach'.

He retired due to ill health in 1947, aged 63, having worked for fifty-one years. Dai (as he was called) died in 1957, aged 73.

A YOUNG BOY recalled the huge and fiery furnaces, the red-hot ingots, the black plates being doubled by tongs and clogged feet. The men who worked here could drink a beer quicker than you could say the word 'pint'. Before dawn, the noise of the men's clogs would be heard as they walked towards the works as Tabernacle clock struck 6 a.m. and then the first tram noisily passed over the points at Woodfield Street. In the quiet of a Sunday morning, there were no clogs and trams to be heard at 6 a.m. in Morriston; just the sound of the cockerels and chickens clucking away, and then chapel doors would open to the sound of their harmonium organs and sermons. Today, Cwm Arian, Cwrt Cilmeri and Cwrt Llwyn Fedwen occupy much of the site.

TREHARNE ROAD

THE NEWER IMAGE is of Morriston District Housing Office constructed on the site of Bryn-y-Nant, No. 13 Treharne Road in May 1999. The last resident at this house was Mr Trefor John Morgan and his wife Cecily Susan Morgan who had lived here for more than forty years. The road was often called Pentre Treharne Road or Pentreharne Road – the latter was confused with the Hafod road of the same name. For many years, the founder of Morriston Ladies Choir lived at No. 11 Treharne Road. Her name was Lilian Abbott, and she was a formidable music teacher and an excellent musician. She was born in 1903; nearly the youngest child of ten children, her father being a packer in the tinplate works.

MISS LILIAN ABBOTT taught at St Winifred's School, Swansea for over twenty years. She founded the Morriston Ladies' Choir in 1945 and remained as their conductor until 1968. She was a great friend of Ivor Sims, the founder and conductor of the Morriston Orpheus Choir and not only did she accompany the choir, but she accompanied the Pentrepoeth Boys' Choir under the baton of their music teacher, Ivor Sims. She was a member of the Gorsedd Circle in 1960 in recognition of her contribution to Welsh music and culture. She was known to people as 'Lil', and lived until 1988 (aged 85).

Mike Cotton, the original coordinator of the new Morriston Chamber of Trade, organised a petition against plans to introduce car-parking charges at this car park at Treharne Road in 2011, filing letters of objection to Swansea Council. The Chamber fought hard against Swansea Council and won. Long may the car park at Treharne Road remain free of charge.

UNO AND CASTLE BINGO

THE LAND IN this part of Morriston was originally part of Morriston Pottery, with a kiln located on Clase Road and one on Neath Road. The site was later occupied by Uno Tinplate Containers Ltd at Neath Road and Alpha Containers Ltd at Clase Road, making tinplate containers and cardboard boxes throughout its time there. The Uno was dissolved in August 1985 and, by 1987, it was ready for demolition as the earlier photograph shows. For nearly three years, the site remained cleared with advertisement billboards around the perimeter of the wall. In the early 1990s, Castle Leisure decided to build a £3 million bingo hall on the site, seating 1,200 people and providing entertainment seven days a week with

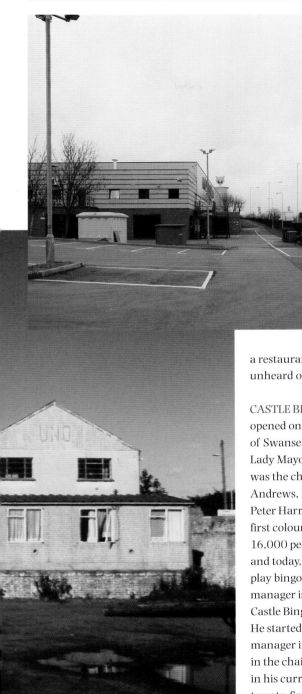

a restaurant facility, which was completely unheard of in the history of Morriston.

CASTLE BINGO IN Morriston was officially opened on 23 March 1993 by the Lord Mayor of Swansea, Councillor Charles Birss and the Lady Mayoress, Mrs Val Pearce. Also present was the chairman of Castle Leisure, Mr David Andrews, his wife Sue and the first manager, Peter Harris. It was advertised as having the first colour matrix screen in Wales. More than 16,000 people signed up to become members and today, many travel from West Wales to play bingo in Morriston. The current general manager is Jason Harries and he is one of Castle Bingo's longest-serving managers. He started in Morriston as an assistant manager in 1996, worked at other bingo halls in the chain, having now returned to Morriston in his current role. Castle Bingo celebrates its twenty-first birthday in 2014.

WELCOME-TO-TOWN

THE EARLIEST RECORDS for the Welcome date back to 1850, but it is said that the pub was much older than this. The last family to run the Welcome, on the corner of Woodfield Street and Lower Slate Street, were the Harris family from 1910 until 1968/69. the Jeremiah family had previously been running the pub and other pubs in Morriston. In the 1860s, John Jeremiah and his wife Sarah Ann started to run the Welcome, after living with John's father at The Bevans Arms. John's eldest sister married Daniel Edwards (*see* Bedford House). The Jeremiahs lived at the Welcome-to-Town until 1907 and in that time John Jeremiah's grandson, Jeremiah Jeremiah, wrote his memoirs about 1900–07.

IT WAS FROM those memoirs that the author has been able to discover the following insights. The time when all the regulars would come together was 8.30 p.m., when the socialising would be at its peak. The collection of men would be anything from

works managers to labourers. In the kitchen would be Jeremiah's father, John Owen Thomas Jeremiah and his friends. In the parlour, or 'commercial room' as it was known, would be the local shopkeepers or tradesmen. In the bar, would one would find mostly tinplate workers and labourers, but absolutely no women at any time – as previously mentioned, women served in pubs but they did not socialise in them.

A regular customer living in Slate Street was Twn Bach Billy Welsh; he kept the landlord's greyhounds and was a barman and cellar man at times. He was a good step dancer, and once won a competition where the prize was 10s (a lot of money in those days). The landlord collected the prize money and gave it to Billy Welsh at sixpence a time. The well-known Morriston pub was victim to the bulldozers in the late 1960s.

WOODFIELD STREET (FROM ST JOHN'S CHURCH)

ENTERING WOODFIELD STREET in 1905 from around St John's Church (in the middle of the road) you would find yourself being greeted on the left by Thomas Davies & Son, ironmongers who filed for bankruptcy in 1922 and Tom Craven, hairdressers and tobacconist who moved here (where Woolworths was originally located) from over the road in 1902. A little further down on the left would be the original location for William Treharne's sweet shop at No. 75; he later moved to No. 80 Woodfield Street. William and his

wife Mary had two children but both died in infancy. Records show that William
(b. 1868) went to work in the tinplate works aged 13 and was still there ten years later.
He died in 1934 aged 67, but his widow Mary lived a further eleven years.

OVER THE OTHER side of the road you would find Isaac Jones (butcher) at No. 56 who in
1902 was fined £1 16s 6d including costs for cruelty to five calves. Ten years later, Isaac
Jones was fined 20s (£1 today) for keeping his shop open after hours. Isaac and his sons
carried out all of their butchery in the slaughter-house on Glantawe Street. In 1911,
the top buildings on the right side of the photo were redeveloped by Mr David Rees,
a plumber of 60 Woodfield Street, whose father, Moses, lived one door down at No. 59.
No. 59 was also the home of Sister Alison Jones who was the minister of Grove Place
Chapel for many years until her sudden death in 1960. The view has not changed all
that much but, of course, the shops have changed over the years.

WOODFIELD STREET
(FROM WELCOME-TO-TOWN)

BURTON ALES INDICATES the Welcome-to-Town public house on the left (No. 40 Woodfield Street) prior to its mock-Tudor appearance. The two-up-and-two-down houses next door were owned by the Welcome and were occupied at various times by greengrocers, sweet shops and fish and chip shops. In 1911, the little house on the end near the wall was occupied by William John Davies (aged 29), his wife Mary Ann, four children and three lodgers all within four rooms (two bedrooms), which would have been a tight squeeze. The railings on the left belonged to the Opera House/Forward Movement Hall and then the tall building, which obscures much of Tabernacle Chapel's tower, belonged to Boots Cash & Co., a boot shop that employed a manager whose family would live above the shop. Today, the left side of the street has been replaced by 1960 block shops, removing all the character that this street once had.

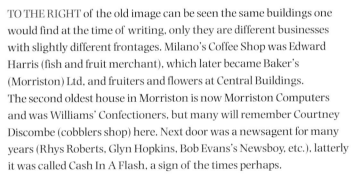

TO THE RIGHT of the old image can be seen the same buildings one would find at the time of writing, only they are different businesses with slightly different frontages. Milano's Coffee Shop was Edward Harris (fish and fruit merchant), which later became Baker's (Morriston) Ltd, and fruiters and flowers at Central Buildings. The second oldest house in Morriston is now Morriston Computers and was Williams' Confectioners, but many will remember Courtney Discombe (cobblers shop) here. Next door was a newsagent for many years (Rhys Roberts, Glyn Hopkins, Bob Evans's Newsboy, etc.), latterly it was called Cash In A Flash, a sign of the times perhaps.

Next can be seen MGK Amusements, which was Walter Tracey Jewellers, a distinguished jeweller who died in 1922. Finally, one can see the tall Anchor House, which was Eastmans Ltd, butchers and purveyors managed by Albert Taylor. Today, the building is occupied by Simply Lush, which sells delicious cakes and baking accessories. The business was started by Leigh Williams in July 2011.

WOODFIELD STREET
(FROM NEAR THE CROSS)

THE BOY IN the 1905 postcard is standing in the middle of Woodfield Street where the cars now queue at the lights of Morriston Cross. On the left of the old image is the end of the whitewashed cottages that were replaced by the art deco, round New Cross Buildings and the purpose-built Morriston Post Office. On the left of the image you can also see Price Jones' home, where he traded as a painter and decorator. The building just out of sight (you can see the large tree in the garden) was referred to in these times as Woodfield House. The previous occupier was Mr William Morris, a tinplate owner who, as an elderly man, laid the

foundation stone for Soar Welsh Baptist Chapel in 1907 (now Sacred Heart Centre). The photo shows Bethania Welsh Baptist Chapel, which opened in 1878, and in the background behind the tram is St David's Church, established in 1891.

AT THE SIDE of the two whitewashed cottages was a lane that is today called Woodfield Lane and it leads to Snooker World. The businesses that could be found past those cottages in the older photo were Joseph Carpenter (confectioner), John Morgan (newsagent), Joseph Thomas (gas producer in steel works), and in the big building where a lady stands outside lived Hywel Preston, a painter who probably assisted Price Jones. Boarding with Hywel was Dr Fellan, a 53-year-old medical doctor from Tipperary in Ireland. Today the building is a newsagent, having once been owned by Alan Hole and rebuilt in the 1960s by Albany's Furniture Shop. The pavements have become much wider here to accommodate the new metro buses nicknamed the 'bendy bus'.

WOODFIELD STREET (NOS 15–20)

NOS 15–17 WOODFIELD STREET opened in these buildings as Peglers Supermarket in around 1969. Peglers did not last long and after it closed, the building was occupied by Handiland DIY shop, long before B&Q ever came to Swansea. When Handiland closed, the employment exchange modernised and, in 1980, it moved into the shop rebranded as the Job Centre. It stayed here for more than thirteen years before moving to the upper part of Woodfield Street and an old face called Peacocks returned once more. Peacocks came to Morriston in the late 1920s as G.W. Peacocks Ltd Bazaar shop, and was situated in the small shop next to Barclays Bank. It later moved up to the middle of Woodfield Street on the site of what is now Iceland. Peacocks moved back in 1993 to its current location.

Nos 18–20 WERE built by Rees & Kirby (Morriston) Ltd and opened on Monday, 6 December 1971 as Batemans Wales and the West supermarket, offering double Green Shield stamps on everything until Christmas Eve. Green Shield stamps were offered for many years by supermarkets for you to collect and exchange as gifts. Argos started up as a Green Shield gift shop. Morriston shoppers then saw International Supermarket replacing Batemans, which was then replaced by Gateway (pictured here in 1986) and then Somerfield. December 2011 saw the building boarded up when Co-op pulled the Somerfield brand out of Woodfield Street and the future of the shop looked uncertain. Fortunately, the boarded up appearance did not last long as Poundstretcher opened in early 2012, beginning a new chapter in the history of this shop. Older readers will remember Oxford Studios, Mathias Stores and two houses on the site of these shops. In conjunction with a £250 contribution made by the people of Morriston via collection tins, the Morriston Chamber of Trade were successful in lighting up the trees here during the Christmas period of 2012; at a cost to the Chamber of over £3,500. It shows that when Morriston people come together, great things can be achieved.

WYCHTREE
BRIDGE

THERE HAS BEEN a bridge over the River Tawe here since
the Middle Ages when pilgrims from East Wales and beyond
used to pass this way on their journey to St David's Cathedral.
Then in 1778, following an Act of Parliament, bridge builder
William Edwards, who was also responsible for planning the
early Morris Town as well as building other bridges including
Pontypridd, built the stone Wychtree Bridge with his distinctive
circular openings in the haunches to relieve pressure on the
arch. The old bridge was built to accommodate horse-drawn
vehicles but ended up supporting far heavier vehicles, especially
during the Second World War when large trailer-lorries, some
with a combined weight of 120 tons, crossed over without any
incident. The bridge, sometimes known as Forest Bridge, was too
narrow and a steel footbridge had to be constructed alongside to
accommodate pedestrians.

THE UPPER FOREST & Worcester Tinplate Works (now the site of Asda) would not give or
sell land for the 1959 bridge (pictured here in 1982) in order for it to be built alongside the
William Edwards' bridge, copying the design of the Pontypridd one, so the 1778 bridge had
to be demolished. Ironically, the works closed around the same time as the new bridge was
completed and 180 years of history was lost. The clearance of the works provided a chance
to extend the once narrow road without a pavement into a dual carriageway. During the
Wychtree underpass construction of 1994, the 1959 bridge was replaced by the one in the
more recent photograph. As can be seen in this image, the landscape in the background
has altered; the Alpha and Uno Works has been replaced by Castle Bingo and the impressive
tower that changes colour all night, every night and the grassed Wychtree roundabout now
looks into the underpass. These changes are ideal examples of how Morriston continues
to evolve.

If you enjoyed this book, you may also be interested in …

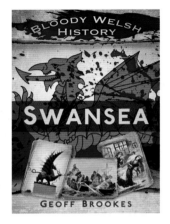

Bloody Welsh History: Swansea
GEOFF BROOKES

Bloody Welsh History: Swansea delves into the city's gruesome past and will ensure that you never look at local history in the same way again … The darker side of Swansea in one handy – and extremely horrible – volume. Geoff Brookes looks at every brutal happening between AD 43 and 1947, including the Battle of Llwchwr, the Rebecca Riots and the wreck of the *Samptampa*. Illustrated with more than seventy black and white illustrations and rare historical images, this is a must have for residents and visitors alike.

978 0 7524 8053 4

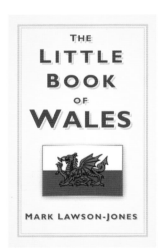

The Little Book of Wales
MARK LAWSON-JONES

The Little Book of Wales is an intriguing, fast-paced, fact-packed compendium of places, people and history in Wales. Here we find out about the country's most unusual crimes and punishments, eccentric inhabitants, famous sons and daughters and literally hundreds of wacky facts (plus some authentically bizarre bits of historic trivia). Mark Lawson-Jones' reference book and quirky guide can be dipped into time and time again to reveal something new about the people, the heritage, the secrets and the enduring fascination of Wales.

978 0 7524 8927 8

Visit our website and discover thousands of other History Press books.

www.thehistorypress.co.uk